A Closer Look at
VIKINGS

A CLOSER LOOK BOOK
© The Archon Press Ltd
1979

Originated and designed by
Charles Matheson
and produced by
The Archon Press
70 Old Compton Street
London W1V 5PA

The author is Lecturer in
Medieval Archaeology,
University College,
University of London.

First published in
Great Britain 1979 by
Hamish Hamilton
Children's Books Ltd
Garden House
57–59 Long Acre
London WC2E 9JL

0 241 10119 0

Printed in Great Britain by
W. S. Cowell Ltd
Butter Market, Ipswich

A closer LOOK at VIKINGS

Helen Clarke

Illustrated by Ivan Lapper

Hamish Hamilton · London
In association with
British Museum Publications Ltd

4

Raiders!

Until the end of the eighth century AD, Scandinavia was a peaceful region, hardly noticed by the rest of Europe. Then, suddenly, the pagan Vikings burst out of Sweden, Denmark and Norway to attack Christian Europe, devastating town and countryside.

The first raid on England took place at Portland on the Dorset coast in *c.* 789. Three ships were greeted by Beaduheard, the reeve (or steward) of the king of Wessex (in southern England), who thought that they belonged to merchants. But the travellers proved to be pirates who murdered Beaduheard. An attack on the monastery of Lindisfarne off the coast of Northumbria (modern Northumberland) followed in 793 and from then onwards the number of attacks increased. People fled in terror whenever they sighted the Viking longships, leaving their homes open to the looting and plundering of the Danish and Norwegian pirates.

The name Viking – which probably means people who come from inlets and creeks but came to mean sea-going pirates – was applied to the Danes, Norwegians and Swedes. The Danes mainly travelled south to raid south-east England, the Low Countries and northern France. The Norwegians sailed westwards to Scotland, the Northern Isles, Ireland and the Isle of Man. The Swedes looked eastwards, across the Baltic Sea to Russia and beyond. Until the middle of the ninth century the Vikings raided Europe in the summers and returned home with their spoils in the winter. Then a change occurred; more and more Vikings went abroad to settle and a new phase of the Viking Age had begun.

From the fury of the Northmen, Oh Lord deliver us

So prayed the Saxon monks when the pagan Vikings descended savagely on their peaceful and undefended monasteries. For two hundred years the monasteries, many of them by the coast or on islands, had built up collections of richly decorated and valuable objects for the glory of God. The Vikings fell upon these, either melting down the gold and silver into ingots or taking precious objects back to their homes as loot. This stone (above) from Lindisfarne graphically illustrates the Viking raid of 793. Britain did not suffer alone. Scotland, Ireland, Frisia (in the Low Countries) and France as far south as the Loire felt the Viking fury.

5

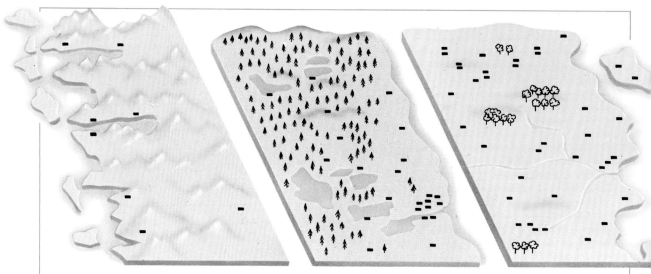

Norway
Farms were situated on the narrow coastal strip of level land beside fjords which cut deep into the countryside (see below).

Sweden
In this country of lakes and pine forests most people lived in the central and southern districts where there was agricultural land.

Denmark
Denmark was low-lying. Forest areas were cleared for arable and pastoral farming to feed the growing population.

A harsh land

The Vikings' own lands were not easy places to live in. In Viking Age Scandinavia most people depended on farming – mainly of sheep, goats and cattle although arable farming was important in Denmark – but they often gained a poor living from the land. As the population began to increase, more land was needed to support it, so in the ninth century many Scandinavians went 'a-Viking', first to raid and then to colonise foreign lands.

Society in Viking Age Scandinavia was strictly divided into classes, as it was in the rest of Europe at that time. In the lowest class was the slave (þraell or thrall) used as labour on the farms. Some slaves were born in Scandinavia but many were brought from western Europe as loot.

The next class was that of the free peasant or karl who either owned his own land or worked the land of his master, an aristocrat or jarl. The jarl was a warrior who commanded 'armies' of free peasants and ruled areas of the countryside in almost complete independence. Above the jarls were the kings who became more powerful as the Viking Age advanced.

The Thing
The Thing was the public assembly of all free men which acted as a court of law. There were local Things and Things which represented larger areas or even whole nations (as the Althing did in Iceland). There was often bitter fighting and feuding among the jarls. The number of beautiful and efficient weapons that have survived from this period show how important warfare and combat were to the Vikings. A fight like the one below, in which a man was killed, would have been judged by the Thing. Often a sum of money had to be paid by the murderer to the relatives of the man he had killed but offenders could also be banished.

7

At home

Inside the house
The rectangular, smoke-filled room was divided into three by upright wooden posts which supported the roof. The hearth lay in the middle strip of floor and the areas between the posts and walls were often built up with earth to form raised benches lined with wood or stone. These were used as beds at night, piled with straw, cloth and furs; in the daytime the bedding would be cleared away and the benches used as working spaces.

At home most Vikings were simple farmers. The loot brought back from summer raiding by Viking menfolk may have been used like money – to provide the means of clearing more land for agriculture or for luxuries like spices and wine from abroad. One of the most important forms of loot was slaves who could be put to work on the farms. The Viking farmhouse was a simple building. The hearth in the middle of the floor provided light and heat for warmth and cooking, the smoke from the wood fire finding its way out through a hole in the roof.

Meals, usually of stewed vegetables and meat, were prepared in iron cauldrons, stone bowls or pottery containers which could be hung on chains or ropes over the fire or, in the case of pottery or stone, embedded in hot ashes. Meat was also roasted on a spit or buried with hot stones in a pit beside the hearth. Mead, a drink based on honey, and a type of beer were the usual drinks but richer families drank wine imported from France or Germany. Drinks were kept in wooden buckets or barrels bound with iron hoops, and drunk out of drinking horns or beakers of horn or wood.

The house was the centre of all other domestic activities, the most important being spinning and weaving cloth out of the wool from the family's own sheep. Wool was spun by hand onto a wooden stick called a distaff or spindle; it was then dyed with colours taken from plants, rocks or earth (green, brown, dark red or yellow) and finally woven into the finished cloth on an upright loom.

Modern dwellings
The Black Houses of the Hebrides continue a tradition of building begun by the Viking colonists of the Northern Isles. They consist of one long room with thick stone and turf walls and a thatched or turf roof.

A second home

The people of Denmark, Sweden and Norway were brought up with boats from their childhood. In Norway and Denmark none of the settlements was far from the sea and in Sweden most inland travel was also by water. The Vikings sailed in ships which were much more advanced than others in Europe at that time. They were the first people in northern Europe to build ships with sails (although there are stones on the island of Gotland, in the Baltic, from before the Viking time which show ships with sails) and this gave them an enormous advantage over the ships of other countries which had oars alone. The Viking ships had oars as well as sails which meant that they could be independent of the wind. The ships were also designed to withstand very rough seas such as the waters of the Atlantic and yet their shallow draught allowed them to sail far inland along rivers and easily to be drawn up on sandy beaches.

The solid oak keels, forming the backbones of the ships, made them strong enough to carry the tall pine masts and the big, square sails. Attached to the keel were overlapping oak planks (called

Dragon ships
The prows of Viking ships were often decorated with brightly painted heads of dragons. The most famous type of ship to carry these figureheads was the longship, an ocean-going warship with a sail and oars which held 70 or 80 men. These were the ships which struck terror into the hearts of the people of western Europe.

Master craftsmen
Viking shipbuilding skill was applied to all sorts of craft from merchantmen to small coastal vessels. The ship being repaired right is a smaller version of the longship based on the elegant, high-prowed Oseberg ship, found in 1903 in a burial mound beside Oslo Fjord. It had belonged to a Viking princess.

strakes) which formed the hull. The strakes were joined together by iron clench nails. The hull was waterproofed by caulking – plugging the gaps between the strakes with animal hair and a coat of pitch. The strake at the waterline was thicker than the others to strengthen the hull against the pressure of the sea and one of the upper strakes was pierced with holes for oars. Then the hull was given shape by ribs which were lashed to the strakes. Cross beams running across the width of the ship served as supports for the deck planks. A heavy piece of timber, the keelson, was laid on the keel. Above this was the 'mast fish' a piece of oak with a socket in it for the mast.

With these beautiful and efficient ships the Vikings sailed great distances. They usually stayed as close to the coast as possible by day and camped on the beaches at night. But soon their skill in shipbuilding and navigation enabled them to sail into the open seas further than ever before, out of sight of land, and they travelled safely to Iceland, Greenland and America across the stormy Atlantic Ocean.

Towns and trade

Hedeby

Hedeby began as an unwalled settlement protected by a fortress to the north. Its earth and wood wall, with three gateways, north, south and west, was built in the tenth century. To the east was the harbour, defended by a wooden palisade. The centre of the town was where a small stream flowed into the harbour. Wooden houses lay in small fenced plots of ground with their gables facing the wood-paved streets. Merchants and craftsmen lived in the houses. Craftsmen made everyday objects (bowls, combs, beads, shoes, jewellery and so on) for the inhabitants of the town and for export by the foreign merchants who visited Hedeby during the two hundred years of its existence.

The Vikings were not only farmers, pirates and warriors, they were traders and craftsmen too. About AD 800 long-distance trade in luxury goods began to increase in importance and amount. Trade routes stretched from the British Isles in the west to Baghdad or even further in the east. Silk, spices, and above all silver were carried from the east along the rivers of Russia to the Baltic Sea and then to newly-founded market centres in Scandinavia. Thousands of silver coins, many from Byzantium and the Arab world, have been found in Scandinavia where they were prized by the Vikings for their silver content not their face value, as the Vikings did not use coins at that time. In return, the Vikings exported precious furs, amber, walrus ivory, iron objects such as sword blades, and slaves.

The market centres began to develop into towns at the beginning of the ninth century. In Sweden the town of Birka, on an island in Lake Mälaren, dominated eastern trade. In Jutland, Denmark, two towns developed at roughly the same time. Ribe near the west coast first grew up as a market for cattle which were exported to Germany. It was soon overtaken in importance by Hedeby (also

known as Haithabu) which grew to be the largest Scandinavian town in the Viking Age. In the tenth century it was surrounded by a huge semi-circular wall of earth and wood. In its rectangular wooden houses lived merchants – from the British Isles, the Low Countries, France, the Baltic lands, Russia, even Arabia – and craftsmen, workers in wood, bone, amber, leather and metal.

All three towns were thronged with merchants, Scandinavians and foreigners, but there were smaller market centres too, like Kaupang in eastern Norway where farmers traded local products, and Paviken on the Island of Gotland (a shipbuilding centre). In the tenth and eleventh centuries, a second generation of Viking towns grew up, particularly in Denmark (Aarhus, Viborg, Lund). These towns survive to the present day; the sites of the earlier towns are mostly deserted now.

Units of trade
Coins and jewellery were often chopped into small pieces and valued for their weight.

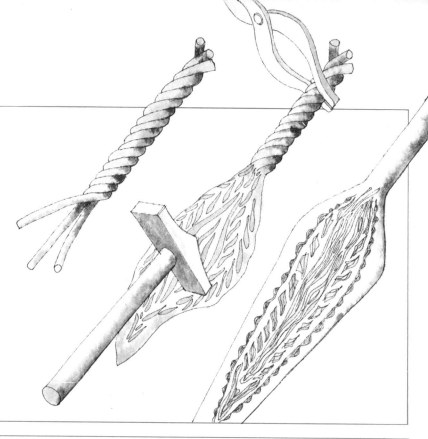

Forging swords and spears

Swords and spears were made of iron by a method known as pattern-welding. Thin rods of iron which contained varying quantities of carbon and phosphorus were welded onto the surfaces of a simple iron core. Then the cutting-edges of high quality steel were welded to the edges and the whole sword or spear polished and ground to show up the pattern on the surface and sharpen the edges. This method produced weapons which were strong, flexible and beautiful to look at. Some were inlaid with names, patterns or symbols which would bring good luck in battle to the owner.

Cauldrons and gridirons

Cauldrons used in cooking were made of sheets of iron riveted together into a bowl-shape; an iron rim was fastened around the top and a semicircular handle was attached to it. Gridirons made of strips of iron coiled into a spiral may have been used for grilling meat.

Scales

Scales or balances for weighing precious metals were carried by most merchants on their travels around the trade routes of the Viking world. They could be folded and kept in a small round case when not in use. Scales like these have been found in the Viking towns of Birka and Hedeby.

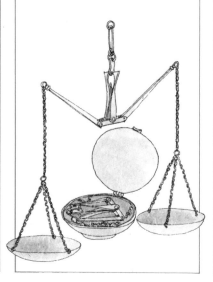

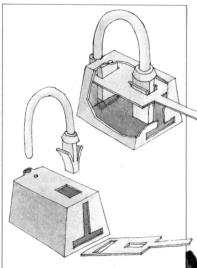

Padlock

The padlock's locking mechanism consisted of a curved iron shackle with strips called leaf springs at the end. The lock was opened by inserting a key in the T-shaped slot and pushing it up to press the leaf springs together. Then the whole mechanism could be lifted out.

Art and artifacts

Viking craftsmen were skilled in making jewellery, weapons and objects of everyday life. They either lived in towns like Hedeby which had specialised craftsmen quarters and a market where they could sell their wares, or they travelled around the countryside from farm to farm, making new things or repairing old. The blacksmith and carpenter, in particular, very often travelled in this way and we still have the tool chest of one such craftsman (who was both blacksmith and carpenter combined). He must have dropped the chest as he was crossing a lake in Gotland around the year AD 1000.

The jewellery worn by Viking women and the weapons carried by Viking men are often very highly decorated with elaborate animal patterns. The animals are stylised (not very like real animals) and closely intertwined, so it is sometimes difficult for us to understand the patterns today. But most of the animals are four-legged and perhaps are derived from a horse.

A great deal of Viking Age art must have been carved in wood, but unfortunately most of this has not survived, so we must rely on work in materials like bronze, silver, iron, ivory and horn to show us the styles and skills of the craftsmen of the Viking Age.

Bone, horn and antler
These materials were used to make spoons, knife handles, spinning, weaving and sewing equipment and, above all, combs. A narrow, curving strip of red deer antler (easily found in Scandinavian forests) formed the back of the comb. The teeth were cut from rectangular plates of antler joined to the back by bronze pins. The combs were often carried in cases also made of antler.

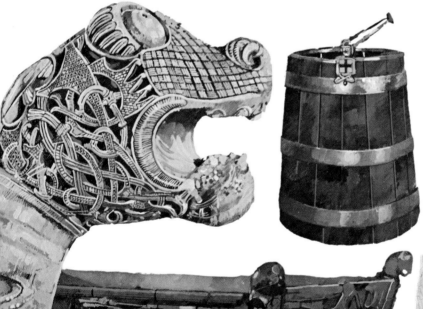

Wood
Viking woodworkers used iron tools like axes to cut down trees, iron wedges to split the trunks, and adzes to shape them. They used iron chisels, drills and spoon bits to decorate their work. Everyday objects like buckets were often left undecorated but the bed, sledge and one of the animal-head posts from the royal ship burial at Oseberg in Norway are elaborately decorated.

15

In search of new lives

In ninth-century Scandinavia it became more and more difficult to feed the growing population, particularly the families of younger sons who inherited no land of their own. So the more adventurous Vikings went to find new lands across the seas.

Norwegians and Danes first began to settle in western Europe where they often had to win their possessions by force. From about 800 onwards the Norwegians also sailed further westwards – to Shetland which is only 320 kilometres or 48 hours sailing from Norway – to Orkney, the Hebrides and the west coasts of the British Isles. Many of the places were uninhabited so the Norwegians could settle down without bloodshed in places which often looked quite similar to home but where they could grow better crops and generally live more comfortably. In about AD 870 Norwegians began to sail further afield and to discover new lands – Iceland, Greenland and North America.

Other Vikings travelled further south. By the middle of the ninth century they had come into conflict with the Moors who then ruled Spain, and in 860 there was a Viking fleet in the Mediterranean. However, the Vikings did not make any permanent settlements in these regions. Their most southerly colony was Normandy.

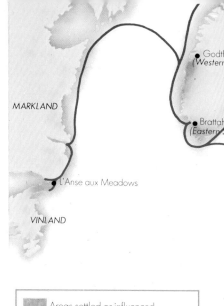

MARKLAND

Godthå
(Western

Brattahl
(Eastern S

L'Anse aux Meadows

VINLAND

Areas settled or influenced

Trade and plunder routes

Scale in Kms

0   100   200   300   400   500

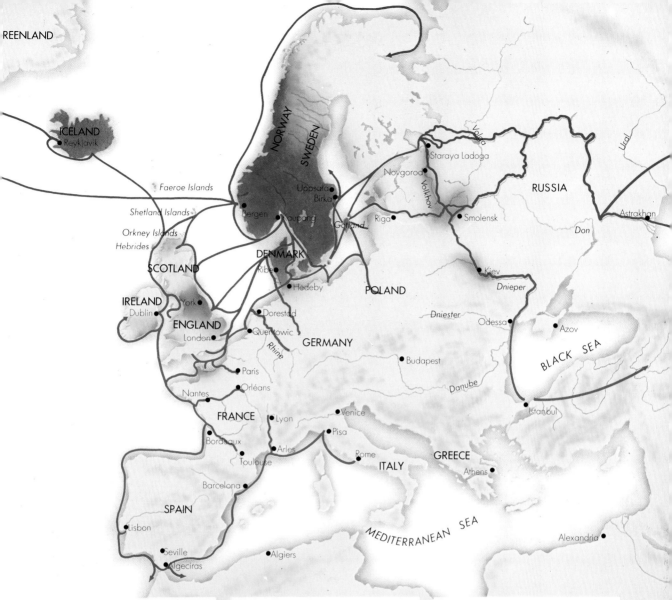

REENLAND

ICELAND
Reykjavik

Faeroe Islands

Shetland Islands

Orkney Islands

Hebrides

SCOTLAND

IRELAND York
Dublin

ENGLAND
London

NORWAY

SWEDEN

Uppsala
Birka
Bergen Kaupang Gotland

Staraya Ladoga

Novgorod

Volkhov

Volga

Ural

RUSSIA

Astrakhan

Riga

Smolensk

Don

DENMARK
Ribe
Hedeby

POLAND

Dorestad
Quentowic

Rhine

GERMANY

Kiev

Dnieper

Dniester Odessa

Azov

BLACK SEA

Paris
Orléans

Nantes

FRANCE Lyon

Bordeaux

Toulouse

Arles

Barcelona

SPAIN

Lisbon

Seville
Algeciras

Venice

Pisa

Rome

ITALY

Budapest

Danube

GREECE

Athens

Istanbul

MEDITERRANEAN SEA

Algiers

Alexandria

We call no man master, we are all free men

Many of the Icelandic settlers (left) were chieftains from south-west Norway and their followers. They moved from their homeland to escape the new king, Harald Fairhair, who by about AD 900 had the whole of Norway under his rule. Before that time the lords of the different parts of Norway had almost been kings themselves, and they did not want to lose their independence. So when they reached Iceland they set up a republic and a parliament, the Althing, which met every summer at Thingvellir. They remained independent from Norway until the 13th century.

Icelandic saga

Sagas and histories tell us a great deal about the settlement of Iceland. Ingolf, a Norwegian, first settled there c. AD 870 at Ingolfshöfði (Ingolf's head) south of modern Reykjavík. He was followed by other Norwegians over the next 50 or 60 years. We know the names of some of the most important settlers from *Landnámabók* (The Book of Settlements). The country seemed rich and prosperous to the first settlers, with pastures for animals 'dripping with butter', land to grow a few crops, birch forests for fuel and building, and large deposits of iron ore in the lakes and bogs.

Rollo and Normandy

In 911 Rollo and his Danish army were given Normandy by Charles the Simple, king of France. Rollo had to promise to defend the land entrusted to him by paying homage to Charles. At the ceremony, Rollo was to kneel and kiss Charles's foot. Instead, Rollo reached down and dragged the king's foot up to his mouth. His action was in keeping with the character of the Danish Vikings of Normandy who were reluctant to admit that any one of their own number ruled over them, let alone that they owed loyalty to a foreign king. When they were challenged to state their leader they cried, 'We are all equal'.

Settlement of Britain

Battle

When the Viking army arrived in England it plundered the Anglo-Saxon villages for horses to ride in battle, and for cattle and grain for food. The Viking army (often called 'here' in Anglo-Saxon descriptions) was on the whole more effective than the Anglo-Saxon 'fyrd' because the Vikings were professional fighting men who made their living as soldiers during the summer. They were splendidly equipped with swords, shields, axes and bows and well trained. The Anglo-Saxons were mustered from the retainers of the king and his lords. They fought from personal loyalty and were very likely to desert once their own leader was killed. They were farmers and peasants, more anxious to be back home in time for the harvest than to die gloriously in battle.

The earliest Viking settlements in Britain were founded in the north and west by Norwegians who from the beginning of the ninth century settled near the coasts of the islands and mainland of Scotland. The Isle of Man and Ireland were also colonised by Norwegians. In Ireland they built strongpoints around the coast which they defended against the native Irish living inland. These places were the forerunners of the modern towns of Dublin, Cork, Limerick, Waterford and Wexford and the Vikings do not seem to have tried to settle further afield. Their strongholds were used as bases for attacks against the Irish and also for raids across the Irish Sea to the west coasts of England and Wales. In the Isle of Man the Vikings appear to have mixed more with the Celtic Christian population and soon took up their religious beliefs.

In all these places the Vikings had begun by acting as pirates and raiders but soon became peaceful farmers and fishermen. They continued to live their lives much as they had in Norway, building the same types of houses, growing the same sorts of crops and, above all, speaking the same language as their relatives at home. Their language, known as Old Norse, was the ancestor of modern Norwegian, Danish and Swedish. Many places in north and west Britain were given their names by the Norse settlers and even today many place names there sound Scandinavian rather than English.

In south and east England, which was split into many kingdoms ruled by Anglo-Saxon kings, it was the Danes who took over the land. By the middle of the ninth century the sporadic raids had stopped and the Great Army of the Danes came instead. By 870 the whole of Anglo-Saxon England roughly north of a line from London to Chester was under Danish control. The Great Army then turned against Wessex, at that time ruled by king Alfred, forcing the king to flee. It looked as if the whole of England would be overrun by the victorious Danes.

19

Danelaw

Alfred the Great
Alfred ruled as king of Wessex from 870 to 899. Although he was at first forced to hide in the marshes of Athelney in Somerset, he soon began a campaign against the Danes that first secured his own kingdom and then, with the aid of an improved Anglo-Saxon army and a fleet, contained them in the area of the Danelaw.

In 878 king Alfred was able to raise an army among the men of Wessex. He fought victoriously against the Danes and saved the kingdom from their domination. A treaty between Alfred and the Danes in 886 allowed the Danes to occupy legally that area of England which they had already won by conquest – an area which became known as the Danelaw because it was ruled by Danish laws and customs.

The Danes founded some new towns in the Danelaw, the best known being the 'Five Boroughs' of Stamford, Lincoln, Leicester, Nottingham and Derby. The Danish soldiers soon turned into farmers and mixed with the Anglo-Saxon population. They have left their names behind in the hundreds of place names which crowd the eastern and northern counties of England to this day – names like Grimsby (the village of Grim – a personal name). The Danish soldiers settled down and married Anglo-Saxon wives.

At the end of the tenth century and the beginning of the eleventh the Danes and Norwegians began another series of attacks on the east and south of England. The Anglo-Saxon king, Ethelred the Redeless (or Unready) tried to persuade the attackers to stay away

The British Isles
Shaded areas show extent of Viking settlement.

Orkneys — Kirkwall
Hebrides
SCOTLAND
Lindisfarne
Jarrow
Wearmouth
IRELAND
Isle of Man
DANELAW
York
Stamford Bridge
R. Humber
Dublin
Grimsby
Limerick
Chester
Lincoln
Nottingham
Derby
Waterford — Wexford
Leicester
Stamford
Cork
Thetford
WALES
Maldon
WESSEX
London
Winchester
Canterbury
Portland
Pevensey — Hastings

20

by giving them huge sums of money – Danegeld – but the only result was that more and more Danes arrived to blackmail the English king by raids or threats of raids. The thousands of Anglo-Saxon silver coins which have been found in all three Scandinavian countries show that Swedes and Norwegians were with the Danes and they all took Danegeld home as loot.

Finally, Svein Forkbeard, king of Denmark, led an invasion of England which forced Ethelred to flee the country in 1013, and Svein became king of England, only to die five weeks later in February 1014. He was succeeded by his son, eighteen-year-old Knut (Canute) who ruled both England and Denmark as the Anglo-Danish Empire. This lasted until 1042 when, on the death of Hordaknut (Harthacanute), Knut's successor, England was once again ruled by an Anglo-Saxon, Edward the Confessor.

Even after this the Vikings continued to raid England. In 1066 the Anglo-Saxon king Harold Godwinsson defeated the Norwegian king Harald Hardrada at Stamford Bridge in Yorkshire, before himself being defeated by William the Conqueror at the Battle of Hastings. As Normandy was a Viking kingdom, the Norman invasion was in fact the last successful colonising raid by a Viking fleet.

Knut the Great

When his father Svein Forkbeard died in 1014, Knut had to fight for the English throne but once established as king he ruled firmly but justly until his death in 1033. He treated England as his kingdom, not a colony, sending the great fleet back to Denmark, and he established an international reputation for himself as a strong European ruler.

Adventures in the west

Hunting in the far north

Despite its name (given by Erik the Red to encourage settlers) Greenland was an unfriendly country. Much of the interior was covered with glaciers and the only land suitable for habitation was on the south and west coasts. Even there it was impossible to grow crops for food and the Greenlanders relied on cattle and sheep farming for most of their livelihood. But the sea was rich in fish, seals, walrus and whales. Fish were caught with nets or lines and whales were driven from the open sea into inlets where they were slaughtered on the beaches with spears and harpoons. The furs from seal, ivory from walrus tusks, and whalebone were exchanged by the Greenlanders for the goods which they badly needed for survival, mainly corn and timber brought from Iceland and Europe.

The Vikings' strong and seaworthy vessels and their skill in navigation (they may have used a primitive form of compass known as a bearing-dial) enabled them to sail far westward across the Atlantic. Iceland was colonised during the ninth century and then, towards the end of the tenth century, Erik the Red fled there from Norway 'because of some killings'. About AD 980 he had to leave there too, probably for the same reason. He sailed west and discovered Greenland, building himself a farm there. There were probably Eskimos in northern Greenland at this time but the Vikings settled unoccupied land to the south. He encouraged others to go there from Iceland and three groups of farms were founded there known as the East, the West and the Middle Settlements.

From Greenland it was only a short voyage to America, which was first sighted by Bjarni Herolfsson, a Norwegian, in about AD 985 but he did not land. That feat was left to Leif Eriksson (son of Erik the Red). Leif called the lands he visited Helluland (Flatstone Land), Markland (Wood Land) and Vinland (Wine Land). Archaeological excavations at L'Anse aux Meadows in Newfoundland have uncovered traces of the Vikings but there is little evidence that they lived in America for long or explored further than the coasts of modern Newfoundland.

Driven from Vinland by Indians
The first Viking settlers in Vinland called the Indians 'Skraelings' (perhaps meaning 'uglies' or 'screechers') and at first they traded with them. But after three winters trouble broke out and after some bloody battles the Vikings were driven out of Vinland never to return.

23

East to Mikligarðr

The Vikings' chief interest in the east was trade. Boats carrying furs, walrus ivory and slaves from Sweden sailed across the Baltic Sea to the Gulf of Finland, and then along the great rivers of Russia to the lands bordering the Black Sea and the Caspian Sea. They returned from there laden with the luxuries of the east: silk, spices and silver.

Two main routes were used: the western one along the rivers Volkhov and Dnieper to the Black Sea and finally to Byzantium (modern Istanbul, known in Old Norse as Mikligarðr); the eastern route following the River Volga to the Caspian Sea – Baghdad could then be reached by camel train across the desert. In many places shallows or rapids made the rivers impassable so that the boats had to be taken out of the water and hauled overland on rollers, or even carried, until the next navigable part was reached.

Towns grew up along the western route, to control the trade and to give shelter to the Vikings travelling along the Volkhov and Dnieper with their wares. The modern cities of Novgorod, Kiev and Smolensk are some of the towns thought to have been founded by the Vikings, who are called the Rus or Varangians in the early histories of Russia. In 860 or 862 three brothers of the Rus (Scandinavian) people are supposed to have gone to Russia at the request of the native Slavs, 'to restore order and to rule over them'. Rurik, the best known, settled in Novgorod and took control of the surrounding countryside which from then on was known as the 'land of the Rus' (modern Russia). He was the first of a dynasty of princes of Viking descent who ruled in cities such as Novgorod and Kiev until the eleventh century. In about 1030, prince Yaroslav of Kiev married Ingigerd, daughter of Olaf Skötkonung, king of Sweden. At about the same time Yaroslav welcomed to his kingdom Harald Hardrada, the future king of Norway. With these two actions he was continuing the tradition of close contact between Russia and Scandinavia which had started in the ninth century.

The Swedish Vikings who travelled in the east were not all princes or peaceful merchants. Some went as mercenary soldiers to the court of the Byzantine Emperor where they formed his bodyguard. They were known as the Varangian Guard and by some as 'axe-bearing barbarians'.

The Swedish Vikings, both merchants and warriors, have left some memorials of their travels. Excavations in the town of Staraja Ladoga in Russia at the mouth of the River Volkhov have uncovered some wooden buildings which might have been built by the Vikings, and some objects of Scandinavian type including a wooden plank carved with runes (the letters of the Norse alphabet). At Gnezdovo near Smolensk a cemetery of between three and four thousand graves has produced some burials containing grave goods (objects placed in the graves probably to help the dead in the next world) which include Viking swords and jewellery. In Sweden itself, runes carved on stones in the tenth and eleventh centuries tell of travellers who died in Greece (Grikkland to the Vikings) and in the cities of Russia.

The Varangian Guard

The bloodthirsty Viking raiders of the ninth century were the ancestors of those who served as soldiers of the Byzantine Emperor in the tenth and eleventh centuries. They went first as small, independent bands willing, for a price, to fight against the enemies of Byzantium in Crete, southern Italy and elsewhere in the east Mediterranean. But by about AD 1000 they had become organised into the famous Varangian Guard, the crack soldiers of Byzantium and the Emperor's bodyguard, feared all over Europe.

Kings, jarls and skalds

The Viking king had to be a brave and fearless warrior who could defend his country by leading his men in battle at home or abroad. He was supported by his picked fighting companions, the hird, who were richly rewarded for their loyalty. He also had the final decision in matters of law and acted as a sort of priest, an intermediary between his subjects and the gods.

Only slightly less important than the king were the jarls (earls or lords), men who ruled almost like kings over parts of the country and who in many cases felt that they were independent of the king himself. Feuds between the jarls were common, and much of life in the Viking Age was taken up with battles and skirmishes among the Vikings themselves.

The king's court was in no fixed place, but was wherever the king happened to be at any time. The retinue who travelled with him could include his hird, the loyal lords and their families, and skalds (poets). Poets were important members of society, paid professional men who served either kings or lords. They composed poems in praise of the brave deeds of their employers, acting as entertainers at great banquets. The Sagas, which were written down in the thirteenth century, have preserved for us some of the stirring tales of gods and heroes which thrilled the Vikings during the long, dark evenings of the Scandinavian winter.

The battleaxe
The axe was the symbol of the Viking warrior. This beautiful axe from Mammen in Jutland has a silver pattern of a lion entangled in foliage inlaid on it. Such an object must have belonged to a great jarl or even a king.

At court
The king and his hird travelled from one royal farm to another feasting and drinking.

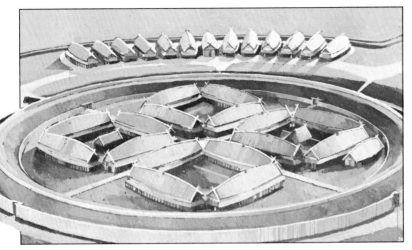

Royal fortresses
Four fortresses like this one at Trelleborg have been found by Danish archaeologists. They have a circular bank with a ditch outside it and entrances at the four points of the compass. The interior of each fort is divided into four by roads running from the entrances and there are four buildings in each quarter. Their geometrical plan gives the forts a very military look. They were probably built to control the areas of country-side round about them, rather like later castles.

Hammer versus cross

Runes

Runes were the letters of the Viking alphabet. They were invented in the lands outside the Roman Empire at about the birth of Christ; some of the runic letters were copied from letters of other alphabets, some were made up. In Viking Scandinavia the runic alphabet had 16 letters and is known as the futhark from the sounds of its first six letters. Runes were probably designed to be carved in wood but we know most about them from rune-stones, found mainly in Sweden where there are more than 3,000. These stones are either tombstones or stones set up to mark roads, bridges or trackways. They are often beautifully carved, usually with a slender snake forming a border to the stone, and were picked out in black, red and white paint. The stone below from Norra Åsarp, Västergötland, Sweden, was raised by Guve in memory of his son Olav, 'A young man active and able. He was killed in Estonia.'

The Vikings worshipped many gods, the three most important being Odin, Thor and Frey. Odin, leader of the gods, was god of kings, jarls and warriors; Thor, with his hammer, was popular with the common people; Frey was the god of fertility. Many myths and legends were told about the gods. Most religious ceremonies in their honour seem to have taken place in the open air with feasting and the sacrifice of animals. The gods were also worshipped in temples of some sort. They may have been ordinary farms but there were also special buildings which housed statues of the gods. No buildings of this kind remain standing today. We know about one of them, near modern Uppsala in Sweden, from a description written by a Christian priest, Adam of Bremen, in about 1070.

The Viking heaven was called Valhalla. This was where the gods lived and where great and brave warriors would go after death. To help him on his way to Valhalla, a rich Viking might be buried in a boat or waggon or in a wood-lined chamber (as in the picture below) with his horses and weapons beside him. Food and drink were also put in the grave, and sometimes a slave might be sacrificed with his master. A Viking warrior might also be cremated on a funeral pyre with his weapons, and ashes and weapons later buried in a pit and covered with a mound of earth or stones. The graves were usually close to the farms where the dead Vikings had lived, and the living may have thought that the spirits of the dead would protect them and their lands.

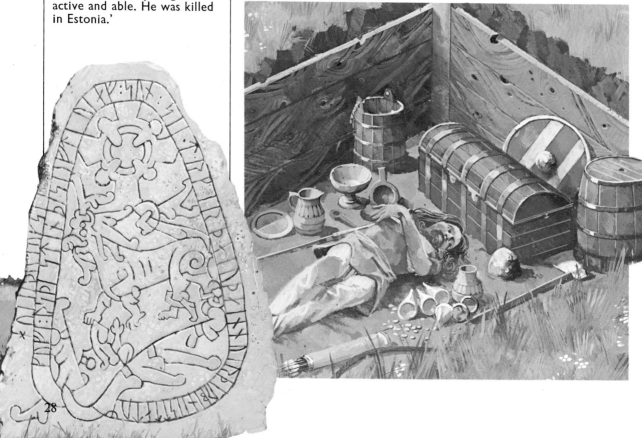

Scandinavian stave churches

The first churches were built of upright planks (staves) and usually had a rectangular nave and a smaller rectangular chancel (where the altar stood). In the eleventh century the churches were small but later they developed into elaborate buildings, some of which (like the one shown here) survive in Norway today.

Hammer and cross

About AD 983 Harald Bluetooth, king of Denmark from 940 to 985, set up a carved stone at Jelling, Jutland, in memory of his parents, Gorm and Thyra. On the stone Harald is described as 'That Harald . . . who made all the Danes Christian.' Norway was forcibly converted to Christianity by king Olaf Tryggvason about AD 1000, but it was the king and saint Olaf, 1016–1030 (portrayed below on an Irish reliquary) who finally imposed Christianity permanently on all Norway. Sweden remained pagan until the twelfth century. Pagan beliefs generally were abandoned only gradually. The Thor's hammer, a pendant worn to bring good luck, was finally changed in favour of the Christian cross.

29

The last Vikings

The last Vikings

The Viking Age in Scandinavia and Europe came to an end in the eleventh century. There was no single dramatic event which caused this, but once all three Scandinavian countries became Christian, they also became much more closely linked with the rest of Europe. European styles of art, architecture and social organisation replaced the old Viking ones. However, Viking traditions lived on in Greenland until much later. From the beginning, the Scandinavian settlers in Greenland relied on imports of grain and timber. For most of their food they depended on sheep, cattle and hunting – which also provided them with their main exports, furs, skins and walrus ivory, which they could trade with Europe. So great was their need for imported supplies that until the fourteenth century the king of Norway sent a boatload of things every year. After the union of Iceland and Norway in 1260, the Greenlanders were forbidden to have their own ships. But Greenland was a long way from Norway and was easily forgotten when Norway itself fell into financial difficulties. The last Norwegian cargo vessel visited Greenland in 1369. After 1200 the weather had become much colder and the amount of ice increased. The Eskimos, better equipped to live in the colder conditions, began to press in on the settlement and there were some bloody battles between them and the Greenlanders. Faced with a colder climate, lack of food and raw materials (particularly wood for building boats), a decline in their numbers and the severing of communications with Europe, the Greenlanders were doomed. The Scandinavian's West Settlement was abandoned by 1340. The East Settlement remained Scandinavian until about 1500 when the last descendants of the Vikings in Greenland finally died out and Greenland belonged to the Eskimos once more.

Index